WEALTH MADE SIMPLE

(yes, really.)

DAVID M RAGLAND

TABLE OF CONTENTS

Author's Introduction

Atlanta, Georgia — Summer, 1996

It's summertime in Atlanta and the Olympics are in town. I've been attending events with friends and family, snapping pictures to memorialize the once in a lifetime event. I rushed to the local drug store to pick up the prints (before the days of digital everything) and I begin flipping through the photos.

After our family dinner that evening, everyone gathered around the table to look at all the pictures. They were awesome; track and field, rowing, baseball events, the venues and all the parties. Everyone laughed and joked about the pictures and about the great times we were all having at the Olympics. I just sat dumbfounded.

Of course I could spot myself in all the photos and I wasn't believing what I was seeing. Was I really that much heavier, okay fatter, than just a few years ago? Waking up every morning and seeing yourself in the mirror you don't really notice the change. Slowly but surely I had put on seventy-five pounds since college and hadn't realized the huge weight gain.

At that moment, I knew I had to make a change. I did not yet know how, but I knew I had to make a change. To me it was simple. I was taking in too many calories every day and because I wasn't exercising, I was gaining weight. I knew that I had to begin exercising and reducing my caloric intake on a daily basis.

Simple, right? Yes. Easy? Not exactly. To date, I have completed sixteen Ironman competitions and it's still simple. I exercise every day and I watch what I eat.

It's simple but it's not always easy.

CHANGE IS ALWAYS
SCARY. THE FIRST
STEP IS SIMPLY THE
DECISION TO MAKE
THE CHANGE.

CHAPTER ONE

 IT'S JUST THAT SIMPLE

JANUARY 2013

I had dinner last evening with an old college roommate. Back in the day, Jeff was the lead guitarist for the local garage band that played for fraternity and sorority socials in Athens, Georgia. Playing these events allowed Jeff to scrape together enough money for tuition and to pitch in and help with the utility bills that kept the heat on during the winter.

Today, it's "Doctor" Jeff and he's a highly respected general surgeon who is the real deal. Forget the TV show "ER"; Jeff is the guy you want if you ever end up on the operating table. Jeff recounted his day operating on an individual, and as he talked about the surgery, all I could think about was *how did he keep everything straight?* Half-way through his story I blurted out, "Man, that sounds really complicated!" He responded, "It's simple if you are doing it right."

The next morning I was meeting with Sarah, a new client who is in the process of "down-sizing" her business. Sarah is happier because she has pared down her employees to herself and a few trusted key players. Sarah is making more money and most importantly, her employees provide greater productivity. What especially caught my attention was what one employee said: "There is no more drama in the office and everything is just simpler."

In our world today it is easy to get overwhelmed. With job, family and the internet, someone or something is always begging for your time or attention. With all that goes on, how can you keep up with the latest and greatest ways to grow your wealth? In my twenty five years of working with individuals and companies in growing their wealth, I have come to find that it is really as simple as this: If you have more money going OUT than coming IN, you are in trouble.

As Dr. Jeff said, "If you are doing it right, it's simple; it's when you are doing it wrong that it becomes complicated."

It's just that simple.

Keys to Wealth Building

> THE SIMPLER YOU MAKE ANY TASK, THE EASIER IT IS TO COMPLETE

> FINANCIAL CLUTTER IS THE ENEMY OF WEALTH ACCUMULATION

If you are doing it right, it's simple.

CHAPTER TWO

FREEDOM

Growing up in a family of six, I am the youngest of four boys. Dinner time came promptly at 6:30 every night and if you wanted to eat you were on time! At an early age, I learned that I was expected to work and to contribute. First, it was household chores (unpaid, of course). Working outside the home for money came next.

My first recollection was helping my older brothers with the neighborhood lawns. I earned a whopping 25 cents for pushing the lawn mower a couple of miles to and from the yards and then emptying the grass clippings from the bag when they became full.

As soon as I was able, I graduated to having my own lawns which increased my income from 25 cents to $3.00 per lawn. Here I first learned of "expense management" and the dreaded TAX MAN! You see, my father required us to pay for our own gas and he also deducted $1.00 per lawn as a "tax" which he collected to fund a new lawn mower every year. Mowing twenty lawns a week required reliable equipment!

At the age of fifteen, I began working at the local Chick-fil-A. There I learned to become a team player and I earned my first real paycheck. While in college, I began working for a bank. Cashing checks, making deposits and opening savings accounts kept me busy during my summer holidays and spring breaks. On Fridays, payday for most people, I would cash checks and pay out more than $20,000.00 in cash. In today's dollars that would be close to $50,000.00! I remember thinking after that first summer that money just became a form of payment and it lost some of its mystery to me.

I was blessed to be able to graduate from college in four years with both my undergraduate degree in accounting and a masters in tax accounting. I was ready to GO! The time had come to get out there and conquer the world without having to listen to my parents. I had been working for fourteen years mowing lawns, working fast food and cashing checks. My time to make some REAL money had arrived!

How quickly my outlook changed. Before graduating, I had loving parents who helped support me throughout college. While working summers, they paid the housing, food, insurance and utilities. My income only had to cover my car and gas. Now I had to cover everything. I realized early that I no longer had to listen to my parents, but I was now working for "the man" nonetheless. I had bills to pay every month and when the alarm clock went off, I did not have a choice of whether to get up or not. I got up!

In 1986, I was facing another forty-three years of working before I could retire at the age off sixty-five.

This was NOT fair! I had already been working for such a long time. At that moment, I dreamed of only one thing: Financial Freedom.

This "freedom" was not a freedom from oppression, racism or discrimination. The "financial freedom" which I dreamed of was the truest sense of freedom. To "own" my life and have the ability to make my own choices was the freedom I dreamed about.

I believed that financial freedom was not just about how much money I had in my bank account, rather a feeling of not having to WORRY about money anymore. At the ripe old age of twenty- two, I set out for the quest to be free— financially free!

Keys to Wealth Building

> FINANCIAL FREEDOM COMES WHEN YOU NO LONGER HAVE TO WORRY ABOUT MONEY

> TRUE FREEDOM IS WHEN YOU ARE IN CONTROL AND MAKING YOUR OWN DECISIONS

CHAPTER THREE

A Plan

As I set out to become financially free, I worked hard, saved money and bought a house. I had no real plans for where I was going. I tried a "shotgun" approach to wealth building which sometimes worked and often times did not. I invested in stocks, bonds, real estate and start-up companies. You name it and I tried it. At the end of ten years I was lost.

Have you seen the commercial with the man walking his dog with the number "$1,759,258" tucked under his arm? The number "$1,759,258" represented the amount of money he would need to save by the time he retired. The man comes across his neighbor who is standing on a ladder trimming his hedges with the number "gazillion" above his head. The dog walker asks his neighbor if a gazillion is his retirement number. "Yes" comes the response. He then asks the most important question of all: "How do you plan for that?" The neighbor's response is "I don't know, I just throw money at it!"

That was me. I was just throwing money into different accounts and investments without any plan at all. How many times have you just thrown money into a retirement account or savings account without any real plan? Becoming financially free does not happen by accident. Creating a plan and being willing to do what it takes to stay with that plan leads to financial freedom.

The process CAN be simple. Having ANY plan is better than having no plan at all! A plan, whether to run a marathon or to reach financial freedom should include three things:

> Goals that you want to accomplish
and by when

> Action steps that you will take to
accomplish your goals

> Progress reports all along the way

Keys to Wealth Building

> A PLAN DRAMATICALLY
INCREASES YOUR
CHANCES OF SUCCESS

> A PLAN KEEPS YOU
ACCOUNTABLE TO
YOUR GOALS

CREATING A PLAN
AND BEING WILLING
TO DO WHAT IT
TAKES TO STAY WITH
THAT PLAN LEADS TO
FINANCIAL FREEDOM.

CHAPTER FOUR

YOUR GOALS
CLEARLY DEFINED

I can remember the moment clearly, as if it happened yesterday. That moment in 1996 when I realized that I was seventy-five pounds overweight. Three weeks after realizing that I had gained those seventy-five pounds, I knew I was working too much and not eating right. The past ten years had led to an ugly result. I was depressed because I knew that I was overweight and I needed to do something about it. I could not seem to get started with anything. Sure, there were many diets out there; however, none seemed to provide me with all the answers I needed.

While watching TV one day (one of my favorite pastimes back then) I happened upon the Ironman Triathlon coverage. I had never heard of the Ironman, let alone a triathlon. The host quickly summarized the race: a 2.4 mile swim followed by a 112 mile bike race and ending with a 26.2 mile run—all in the same day! That was CRAZY! I sat back in amazement for the athletes and what they were about to accomplish while I drank another beer.

Half way through the program, the announcer began a human interest story. The story was about Dick and Rick Hoyt. I listened in amazement. The Hoyts were not just any competitors in the race. Rick had been born with cerebral palsy. Rather than institutionalizing Rick, his parents raised him as a normal child. In that year's Ironman competition, father and son were going to participate.

How was this possible? Dick, the father, was going to swim 2.4 miles towing a raft which carried his son, Rick. Dick would then ride his bike 112 miles with Rick strapped to the front of the bike and finally push his son in a wheelchair for 26.2 miles. The race began at 7:00 A.M. and it took them all day, right up until midnight to cross the finish line. These determined, exceptional athletes finished the race! (http://www.youtube.com/watch?v=flRvsO8m_KI)

At that moment, I had my goal. I was going to participate in an Ironman and cross that finish line. I did not know how I was going to do it, but I did know that I was going to reach my goal. I knew that if the Hoyts could survive the struggles of getting to the starting line and ending up at the finish line, I could get off the couch, lose the weight and cross my own finish line!

I had my goal. I needed my timeline. As it took me ten years to gain the weight, it was going to take some time to get back into shape; therefore, I gave myself two years to complete an Ironman. I had my goal AND I had my timeline.

The first step in obtaining your financial freedom is to determine a clear goal and a timeline to achieve that goal. A clearly defined goal must be measurable and it must be tracked regularly.

Keys to Wealth Building

> SET A SPECIFIC FINANCIAL GOAL

> DETERMINE A TIMELINE TO COMPLETE YOUR GOAL

CHAPTER FIVE

 # DEFINING YOUR GOAL
YOUR NUMBER

When competing in an Ironman, the first thing you realize is that you don't have forever to finish the race! The race begins at 7:00 A.M. and must be completed by midnight. Participants only have seventeen hours to finish the race. I could not imagine completing the 2.4 mile swim, 112 mile bike ride and 26.2 mile run in only seventeen hours! However, I had my goal and I knew that I wanted to complete the event.

With a little help you can determine your financial goals, too. It's simple really. Your retirement number is the amount of money that you will need in order to replace your current income. Said another way, "your number" represents that big pot of money that you will need to carry you through retirement.

"Your number" is the amount of money needed in investable assets (don't include any assets such as your home or personal property) that will produce an income stream large enough to cover bills when you stop working—assuming that you are debt free! To maintain a current standard of living, one will need roughly 100% of current spending. A generally accepted amount needed yearly from one's investable assets would be equal to 4% of the account balance. When determining "your number," consider how long you have to save so that you can determine both "your number" and "your timeline."

When speaking with clients regarding their "number," I am often asked a common question: "Who do you recommend that I use as a professional to help with the number crunching?" My response is always that you should consider having a "financial coach."

Keys to Wealth Building

> Plan to replace 100% of after tax income

> Enlist the help of a financial coach

YOUR RETIREMENT
NUMBER IS THE
AMOUNT OF MONEY
THAT YOU WILL
NEED IN ORDER
TO REPLACE YOUR
CURRENT INCOME.

CHAPTER SIX
YOUR FINANCIAL COACH

I was now ready to begin my journey of becoming an Ironman. I had my numbers: 140 miles in 17 hours and within two years. Yes, I had my destination and my timeline, but now I needed someone to help me get there.

Sometimes you are good and sometimes you are just lucky, as the saying goes. At this point in my life I needed a little luck. Two weeks after beginning my journey of becoming an Ironman, I was invited to a "Lunch and Learn" by a friend. The seminar focus was about healthy eating and exercise. The guest speaker at that lunch was Joe Dillon. I had my bit of luck!

Joe Dillon was a former All-American swimmer, a twice-wounded Vietnam Marine combat veteran and a trainer of 22 Olympic Gold Medal winning athletes. I was so inspired by the program that I knew by following this man's advice and dietary program I would certainly improve my chances of attaining my goal. Joe was my "coach" in those days and with his help I began my journey. *(http://thejoedillondifference.com)*

Some people are good with finances and some people just need a little help. Whether you are great at running the numbers or just need someone to look over your shoulder in developing your plan, a financial coach can be a great asset. A good coach does not necessarily have to be a financial planner. A successful coaching relationship begins with trust. A trusted person that helps you develop your plan and has your best interest at heart is essential.

When looking for a coach, ask yourself the following questions:

> Can I trust that this person has my best interests at heart?

> Is this person financially successful themselves?

> Does this person have a financial background?

> How is your financial services provider compensated?

> Can I count on this person to be around for the long term?

Having a financial coach is not a requirement, but having someone who has already learned the financial planning lessons can dramatically accelerate the learning curve. Your coach should be able to assist you in determining "your number" and a realistic timeline for accomplishing your goal.

HAVING A FINANCIAL COACH
IS NOT A REQUIREMENT,
BUT HAVING SOMEONE WHO
HAS ALREADY LEARNED THE
FINANCIAL PLANNING LESSONS
CAN DRAMATICALLY ACCELERATE
THE LEARNING CURVE.

Keys to Wealth Building

> A FINANCIAL COACH CAN ACCELERATE
> YOUR LEARNING CURVE

> TRUST IS A KEY COMPONENT IN A
> RELATIONSHIP WITH ANY COACH

> WHEN CHOOSING A "PROFESSIONAL" COACH,
> FULLY UNDERSTAND THEIR COMPENSATION

CHAPTER SEVEN

YOUR ACTION STEPS

EAT. TRAIN. SLEEP. It's a simple bumper sticker that I often see when I go to Ironman events. For someone trying to complete their first event, this sticker really sums up the process!

Training for an Ironman takes dedication and a lot of time. If you are like me, then you are working more than 40 hours a week in your "real" job and then scheduling to train for an Ironman as well. A normal training week includes ten thousand meters of swimming, one to two hundred miles of biking and fifteen to twenty-five miles of running. Having a goal is one thing, but having the detailed action plan of when to swim, bike and run is crucial.

Planning to achieve your financial destination also requires a detailed action plan. I believe that the simpler the plan, the greater the likelihood of staying with that plan. Keeping this in mind, we outline the following four action steps as the basis of any successful plan when I meet with a client:

> Spend less than you make
  (save and invest the difference)

> Become debt free

> Protect against unexpected losses

> Maintain a cash safety net

Anyone who has ever gone on a diet knows that creating the plan is simple. Sticking with the plan is the difficult part.

Keys to Wealth Building

SIMPLIFY YOUR ACTION STEPS

> SAVE MONTHLY

> REDUCE DEBT MONTHLY

> PLAN FOR THE UNEXPECTED

> MAINTAIN A CASH SAFETY NET

ACHIEVING YOUR
FINANCIAL GOAL
REQUIRES A DETAILED
ACTION PLAN.
THE SIMPLER THE
PLAN, THE GREATER
THE LIKELIHOOD
OF STAYING WITH
THAT PLAN.

CHAPTER EIGHT

GETTING STARTED

Getting started is always the hardest part of any journey. Ask anyone who has tried to lose weight or begun any worthwhile task and you will find it is the first step that we all fear.

For me, getting started in the Ironman was a daunting prospect. A 2.4 mile swim. A 112 mile bike ride and a 26.2 mile run seemed impossible. How was I ever going to get going?

As any good financial coach will attest, you do not eat the elephant in one bite and you do not become financially free overnight. When beginning my Ironman journey, I found the best way to start was to take an inventory of all of my strengths and weaknesses that could help me on my road to completing the race. I recommend the same exercise before beginning the journey to financial freedom. Clients must take an inventory of their assets (strengths) and liabilities (weaknesses) as a starting point from which to begin.

With your coach's help, you will want to complete the following worksheet designed to help account for assets and liabilities. This practical exercise is the starting point for your journey. The list of assets and liabilities will become your own Personal Balance Sheet.

PERSONAL BALANCE SHEET

Assets   **Current Value**

Cash

   Checking Accounts   _____

   Savings Accounts   _____

                                Total _____

Investments

   Stocks   _____

   Bonds   _____

   Rental Real Estate   _____

                                Total _____

Retirement Savings

   401(k) Plan   _____

   IRA   _____

                                Total _____

Personal Assets

   Residences   _____

   Cars   _____

   Other   _____

                                Total _____

            Grand Total of Assets (A) _____

Liabilities	Current Value
	Net Worth Statement)
Short-Term	
Credit Card Debt	_____
Car Loans	_____
Installment Loans	_____
Total	_____
Long-Term	
Residence Mortgage	_____
Home Equity Loans	_____
Student Loans	_____
Other	_____
Total	_____
Grand Total of Liabilities (B)	_____
NET WORTH (A-B)	_____

Keys to Wealth Building

STARTING IS EASIER THAN YOU THINK:

> **INVENTORY YOUR ASSETS**

> **SUMMARIZE YOUR DEBTS**

> **WRITE IT DOWN**

A SUCCESSFUL
FINANCIAL ACTION
PLAN MUST
DETERMINE THE
AMOUNT OF MONEY
COMING IN VERSUS
THE AMOUNT OF
MONEY GOING OUT.

CHAPTER NINE

Cash In vs. Cash Out

The second step in any successful financial action plan is to determine the amount of money coming in versus the amount of money going out. Whether you use QuickBooks, Quicken, Excel spreadsheets or the back of an envelope, you and your coach should sit down and compare how much money you have coming in after taxes versus your obligations. I recommend going through your bills in detail for an average month to see exactly how your money is being spent.

Your task in this phase of planning is to have enough money left over each month to fund "your number" which you determined when setting your financial goal. Should you have enough excess money to fund your plan, move to the next action step. Should you have more money going out than coming in or if your net positive amount each month is not enough to reach your savings goal, then eliminating or reducing discretionary expenses will be necessary to reach your savings goal. Still short after this step? You and your coach will need to look at ways to adjust your lifestyle and to perhaps reduce some of your fixed expenses. Re-examining your financial goal and timeline might be warranted.

The following personal budget worksheet can be used as a guide to complete this process.

Keys to Wealth Building

> ANALYZE YOUR MONEY COMING
> IN VS. YOUR MONEY GOING OUT

> REDUCE YOUR EXPENSES UNTIL
> YOU CAN SAVE EACH MONTH

> BE WILLING TO MAKE THE HARD
> CHOICES THAT WILL SET YOU ON
> THE PATH TO FREEDOM

> AUTOMATE YOUR SAVINGS

PERSONAL BUDGET WORKSHEET

IN   **Monthly**

After tax wage income   _____

Net rental income   _____

Child or other support income   _____

Other cash income   _____

Total IN (A) _____

OUT   **Monthly**

Mortgage payment (s)   _____

Car payment (s)   _____

Credit card payment (s)   _____

Utilities   _____

Automobile expenses (gas and maintenance)   _____

Insurance (auto, home, life, other)   _____

Clothing   _____

Entertainment   _____

Food (groceries and eating out)   _____

Gifts   _____

Supplies   _____

Travel   _____

Savings plans   _____

Total OUT (B) _____

Monthly Cash Flow (A–B) _____

CHAPTER TEN
How to Save

While training for an Ironman, you quickly fall back in love with activities that you grew up loving. Biking and running come naturally to most people. Even if you have not biked or run around the block in ten years, you quickly remember how to get going due to the intuitive nature of these sports.

The more effort you put into biking and running, the faster you will go. Swimming, on the other hand, is truly all about technique. The harder you push while swimming, generally the slower you will go. Here is where a professional swim coach is invaluable because a coach can show you how to use less effort and learn to swim faster.

Much like biking and running, saving money used to be simple. You spent less than you made and you put your money into a savings account at the local bank. You were paid interest on that money and your money continued to grow.

Today, a saver has many options in the type of accounts (pre-tax versus after tax accounts) for saving, as well as the type of investments (stocks, bonds, options, real estate, etc.)

to consider. Just as in swimming, technique can really help your money grow faster and with less effort.

The best and easiest way to make your savings grow faster is with the help of a retirement plan at work. These plans allow you to put money into a plan "pre-tax" so that you can invest more money into savings each month by not having to pay income taxes on the money. In addition, there won't be taxes assessed on the earnings annually in the plan—another way that your savings can grow more quickly! Some employers provide an incentive for saving by matching some or all of your contributions into the savings plan. This additional contribution is free money! But remember at retirement you will have to pay taxes on the money as you withdraw these funds.

Your financial coach and your professional investment advisor will help you choose the type of account you should have as well as the investment strategies best suited for you. Having a broad based diversified investment portfolio will be a key strategy to follow. I recommend that you and your coach determine your personal risk tolerances and then develop a long term approach to your investing strategy.

THE BEST AND EASIEST WAY TO MAKE YOUR SAVINGS GROW FASTER IS WITH THE HELP OF A RETIREMENT PLAN AT WORK.

Keys to Wealth Building

> MAXIMIZE YOUR RETIREMENT SAVINGS ACCOUNTS FIRST

> DETERMINE YOUR RISK TOLERANCE BEFORE INVESTING

> INVEST BY USING A "LONG-TERM" APPROACH

> MAINTAIN A DIVERSIFIED PORTFOLIO AT ALL TIMES

CHAPTER ELEVEN

SAVING FOR THE LONG-TERM

My Dad used to say that "a picture is worth a thousand words." Boy was he right! What really motivated me to begin my journey 20 years ago was watching an Ironman on television. The excitement of the race and watching athletes of all types crossing the finish line was truly motivating.

Even today I never lose the sense of excitement when I go to Ironman races either to participate or to cheer on a friend who may be racing. For me it is a lifestyle of staying in shape that I hope to accomplish for the next 20 years as well.

Sometimes in getting started, we need a clear picture of what CAN happen to our savings over time. By investing $10,000 today and allowing it to grow over time, the same $10,000 could be worth almost $40,000 in 20 years. This same $10,000 deposit could grow to almost $150,000 in 40 years, assuming a 7% annual rate of return. Someone who begins early in life with a one time savings of $10,000 could see their money grow close to 15 times the original investment.

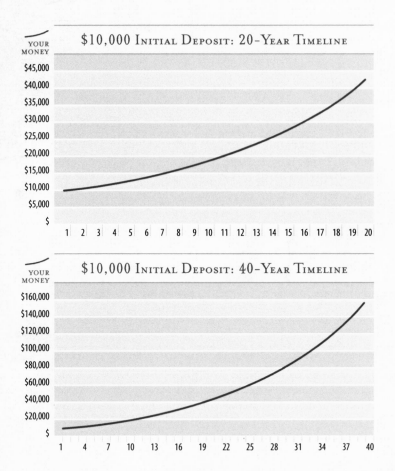

A one-time savings deposit of $10,000 is a great start. As we discussed in the previous chapter, saving regularly using a Company sponsored 401(k) plan or IRA can lead to even higher savings. A person who saves $100 per week in their retirement account could see the account balance grow to approximately $215,000 in 20 years and over $1,000,000 (yes one million!) in 40 years. This example assumes a 7% annual rate of return on the invested savings.

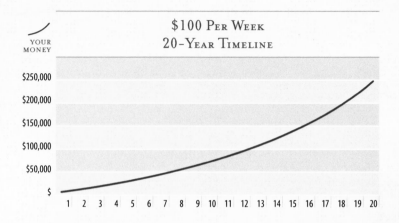

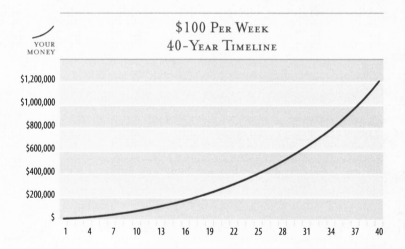

Adding an Employer Match of 50 cents on the dollar to your retirement savings can accelerate your savings even more. Your 20-year balance can grow to almost $320,000 and your 40-year balance can grow to over $1,500,000, again assuming a 7% annual rate of return on the invested savings.

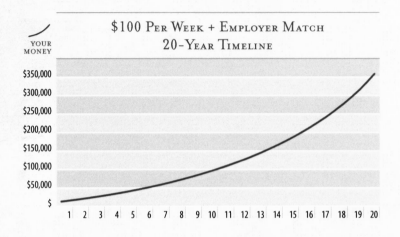

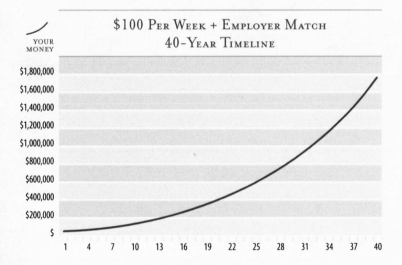

As you can see, "a picture is worth a thousand words." And even better, your savings could be worth more than a million dollars!

Keys to Wealth Building

> > Start early in life

> > Save consistently

> > Remember the power of time and money

CHAPTER TWELVE

LIVING DEBT FREE

According to the United States Federal Reserve Board, the average American family spends an average of 20% of take home pay to fund debt payments. These payments include both consumer and mortgage debt.

A solid long-term financial plan must include a re-payment schedule to become debt free while reaching your financial savings goal as well. Once you are debt free, your ability to live on less income increases dramatically. Remember that in order to pay the debt, not only must you earn the debt payment amount, but also the income taxes to make the debt payments. After adding the taxes owed on income, the average American family spends close to 30% of every dollar earned to pay their debts each year.

When deciding which debt to pay first, I always recommend the following order:

> High interest credit cards

> Non-tax deductible debt

> Home mortgage debt

Consider paying off the mortgage debt last because the interest on your home is usually tax deductible while the credit card debt and other consumer debt is generally not tax deductible.

Keys to Wealth Building

> ADOPT A PLAN TO BE DEBT FREE OVER TIME

> BECOMING DEBT FREE INCREASES YOUR ABILITY TO SAVE

> BY BECOMING DEBT FREE, LESS INCOME IS NEEDED IN RETIREMENT

TRACKING THE
PROGRESS OF YOUR
FINANCIAL FUTURE IS
AS EASY AS TRACKING
YOUR PROGRESS
FOR RUNNING A
MARATHON OR FOR
LOSING WEIGHT.

> Including your coach when reviewing progress

> Making a "to-do list" at each review

Keys to Wealth Building

> Track your progress every six months to your goal with your coach

> On target? Keep going!

> Not on target? Examine what's needed to get back on track

> Those who track against goals see dramatic increases in success rates

CHAPTER FIFTEEN

TRACK YOUR PROGRESS

Now you know where you are going and you have a detailed plan to get there. Now what?

Planning is one thing, but executing the plan is something else entirely. Now that you have a plan, it's time to work that plan! Tracking the progress of your financial future is as easy as tracking your progress for running a marathon or for losing weight.

Since you have a financial picture of where you stand, it's time to track the progress.

Tracking the progress can take any form, but must have some basic components:

> A financial summary of assets and liabilities

> An updated financial summary every six to twelve months

> A consistent time frame such as January 1st and July 1st

WITH A CASH SAFETY NET, IT IS EASIER TO STAY ON PLAN WHEN THE UNFORESEEN EVENTS HAPPEN.

paycheck, you are able to stay on plan. Remember, the three simple steps to financial freedom are:

> Monthly savings

> Debt reduction

> Living a low-risk lifestyle

With a cash safety net, it is easier to stay on plan when the unforeseen events happen.

Keys to Wealth Building

> BUILD A ONE YEAR CASH RESERVE OVER TIME

> A CASH RESERVE KEEPS YOU ON PLAN WHEN UNFORESEEN EVENTS HAPPEN

CHAPTER FOURTEEN

Your Cash Safety Net

Flat tires happen. Life happens.

I was never very good at changing flat tires on my bike. One reason was because I was lucky early on and never got flat tires. As luck would have it, I did get a flat one day while riding with a friend. Not knowing how to change the tire made for an embarrassing fifteen minutes until my friend jumped in and fixed the flat in about two minutes! As you can imagine, today I fix my own flats and I usually help others with theirs, too!

I am often asked why I recommend having a year's worth of cash savings in the bank for unexpected emergencies. Those with more cash liquidity seem to end up with better results in their financial planning than those without the reserves.

Is it just luck? Hardly.

By maintaining a proper amount of cash reserves, should a "bad thing" happen such as needing a new AC unit for the house, fixing the roof or going for a month without a

We all have a level of control over our daily lives and choices. These controls include how fast we drive, where we live or the new job we take. Generally, we are so focused on our work or on our family and friends that we fail to realize the impact of considering the risk versus reward regarding the decisions we make.

As an example, consider your investing philosophy. Do you take a "get rich quick" mentality or a slow, steady approach? A new job may pay you more, but is there a risk of layoff should there be an economic downturn? You can control some of your risks and some of your potential losses. Consider when making your next decision regarding the new job, the next investment or the new anything, that you consider both the reward on the upside as well as the risk on the downside.

Keys to Wealth Building

> REVIEW YOUR INSURANCE NEEDS WITH BOTH YOUR INSURANCE AGENT AND YOUR FINANCIAL COACH

> CONTROL EXPOSURE TO RISKS IN YOUR DAILY LIFE TO STAY ON PLAN MORE EASILY

Planning for something bad to happen did not magically prevent anything from happening, but I was prepared for the events because I had a plan.

When planning for your financial future, plan on saving and paying off debt while also planning for that which might take you off course. Your home is destroyed by fire, you are in an auto accident or you lose the income from a spouse from disability or death—these risks are real. Along with your financial coach you should evaluate self-insuring versus purchasing insurance to mitigate your risks.

Types of insurance you should review with your coach and your insurance agent would include:

> Auto   > Home

> Disability   > Health

> Life   > Umbrella

When reviewing the amount of insurance you might need, it's always best to get the opinions of your insurance agent AND your financial coach. Planning for the unexpected includes getting the right insurance and it also includes trying to live a low risk life. What exactly is meant by a "low risk" life?

CHAPTER THIRTEEN

PLANNING FOR THE UNEXPECTED

The first event of an Ironman race is a 2.4 mile swim. The race begins with a mass start of 2,500 athletes beginning to swim at the same time. The spectators view would appear to be total chaos. From the athlete's prospective, it can be like jumping into a human washing machine. A large school of fish seem to swim magically close together without bumping against each other. As an athlete in this race, you are not so lucky!

I have started races and been kicked in the face, lost my goggles and have had competitors swim over me. At first, I was terrified of the swim. The uncertainty of what "might happen" was always worse than what actually happened.

One day I decided to stop worrying about what "bad things" might happen and instead plan my response should something go wrong. Should my goggles come off then I'd swim the breast stroke. Should I be kicked in the chest, I'd turn over on my back and rest until I regained my breath.

ONCE YOU ARE DEBT FREE, YOUR ABILITY TO LIVE ON LESS INCOME INCREASES DRAMATICALLY.

any debt that you owe. Becoming financially free can be a long journey. The journey takes time and during the process you might be tempted to abandon your plan. The choice is whether or not you want to keep going to reach your own "finish line."

It's simple; it's just not easy.

Well, now you have it. It's time to take the first step. Whether your goal is to become financially free, to become a gourmet cook, or whatever your passion might be, it all begins with committing to the goal. As my Dad always said, "you do not eat an elephant all in one bite." Just take the first bite!

And remember, always enjoy the journey.

CHAPTER SIXTEEN

THE FINISH LINE

Almost twenty years ago I looked in the mirror and decided to make a change. Whether you are trying to lose weight or trying to put your financial house in order, the journey begins with a choice. Going down the same path as before or taking control of your destiny. Change is ALWAYS scary. The first step, as with my Ironman journey, is simply the decision to make the change.

I have finished sixteen Ironman Triathlons to date. One hundred forty miles in one day. Every time I step to the starting line I feel the pit of my stomach churn because I don't know what the day will bring. I have but one destination: The Finish Line. In the end, it is really simple; keep going until you finally get there. Whether getting kicked in the face, enduring the heat or just having your mind tell you to stop, only YOU can make the decision to keep going. It's simple; it's just not easy.

Becoming financially free is simple. Know where you are going, save more than you spend each month and pay off